W9-BHI-673

Reduce, Reuse, Recycle

Water

Alexandra Fix

Heinemann Library
Chicago, Illinois

a division of Reed Elsevier Inc.
Chicago, Illinois

Customer Service 888-454-2279
Visit our website at www.heinemannraintree.com

Designed by Steven Mead and Debbie Oatley
Printed in China by South China Printing Company Limited

12 11 10 09 08
10 9 8 7 6 5 4 3 2 1

ISBN 10-digit: 1-4034-9714-1 (hc) 1-4034-9722-2

Library of Congress Cataloging-in-Publication Data
Fix, Alexandra, 1950-
Water / Alexandra Fix.
p. cm. -- (Reduce, reuse, recycle)
Includes bibliographical references and index.
ISBN 978-1-4034-9714-7 (hc) -- ISBN 978-1-4034-9722-2 (pb)
1. Water conservation--Juvenile literature. 2. Water-supply--Juvenile literature. 3. Water--Pollution--Juvenile literature. I. Title.
TD495.F59 2007
333.91'16--dc22
2007002787

Acknowledgments
The author and publisher are grateful to the following for permission to reproduce copyright material: Alamy pp. **24** (Keith M. Law), **27** (Paul Glendell), **28** (Rob Wilkinson); Corbis pp. **4** (Royalty Free), **7** (Royalty Free), **18** (Carl & Ann Purcell), **21** (Royalty Free), **22** (Royalty Free), **23** (Jean Louis Atlan/Sygma), **26** (Michael Keller); Getty Images pp. **10** (Michael Salas), **11** (Flip Chalfant), **12** (Stone/Paul Chesley), **13**, **15** (Iconica/Ashley Karyl), **16** (Photographer's Choice/Aura), **17** (Taxi/Gen Nishino), **20** (Stone/John Edwards), **25** (Photographer's Choice/Oliver Strewe); Harcourt Education Ltd. p. **19** (Ginny Stroud-Lewis); Science Photo Library pp. **6** (Gusto Images), **9** (Christian Darkin), **14** (Chris Knapton).

Cover photograph reproduced with permission of Alamy/Tim Graham.

Every effort has been made to contact copyright holders of any material reproduced in this book. Any omissions will be rectified in subsequent printings if notice is given to the publisher.

Contents

Some words are shown in bold, **like this**. You can find out what they mean by looking in the glossary.

Why Is Water Important?

Three-fourths of the Earth is covered by water. Most of this water is saltwater from the oceans. Only a very small part is freshwater that we can use in our homes.

The Earth looks blue from space because of water in the oceans and in the air.

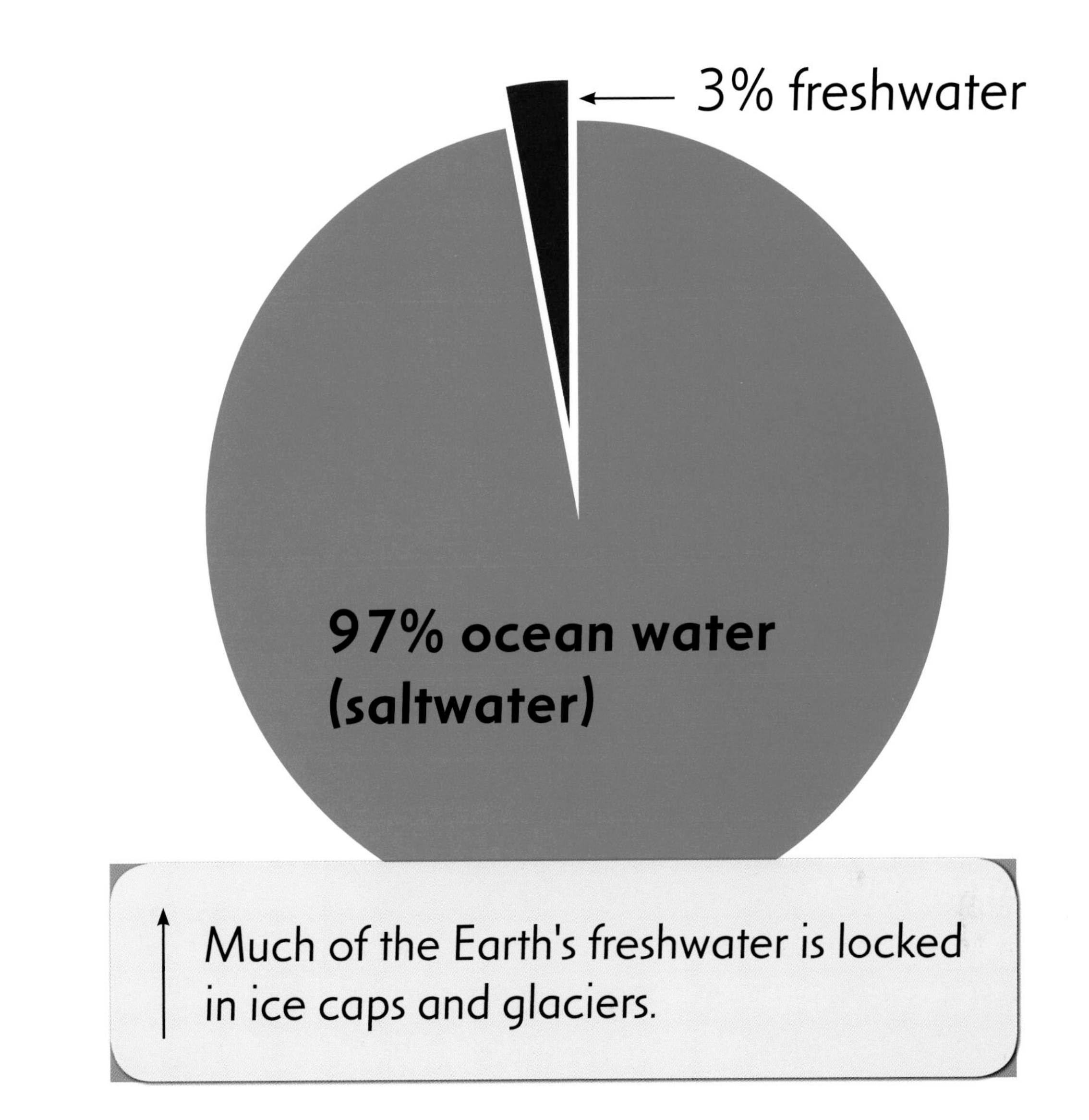

Much of the Earth's freshwater is locked in ice caps and glaciers.

We use water to drink, take showers, clean dishes, and grow food. We need to use water every day, but there are many ways to use less water.

How Do We Use Water?

We need to drink lots of water every day. We also need water to grow plants.

The human body is made up of more than half water.

This power plant uses water to create electricity.

People can use water to make **electricity**. This is a form of **energy** (power) that makes things work, such as the lights in your room.

Where Does Water Come From?

Water is always in motion around the Earth. It changes form, but does not disappear. This constant motion and change is called the **water cycle**.

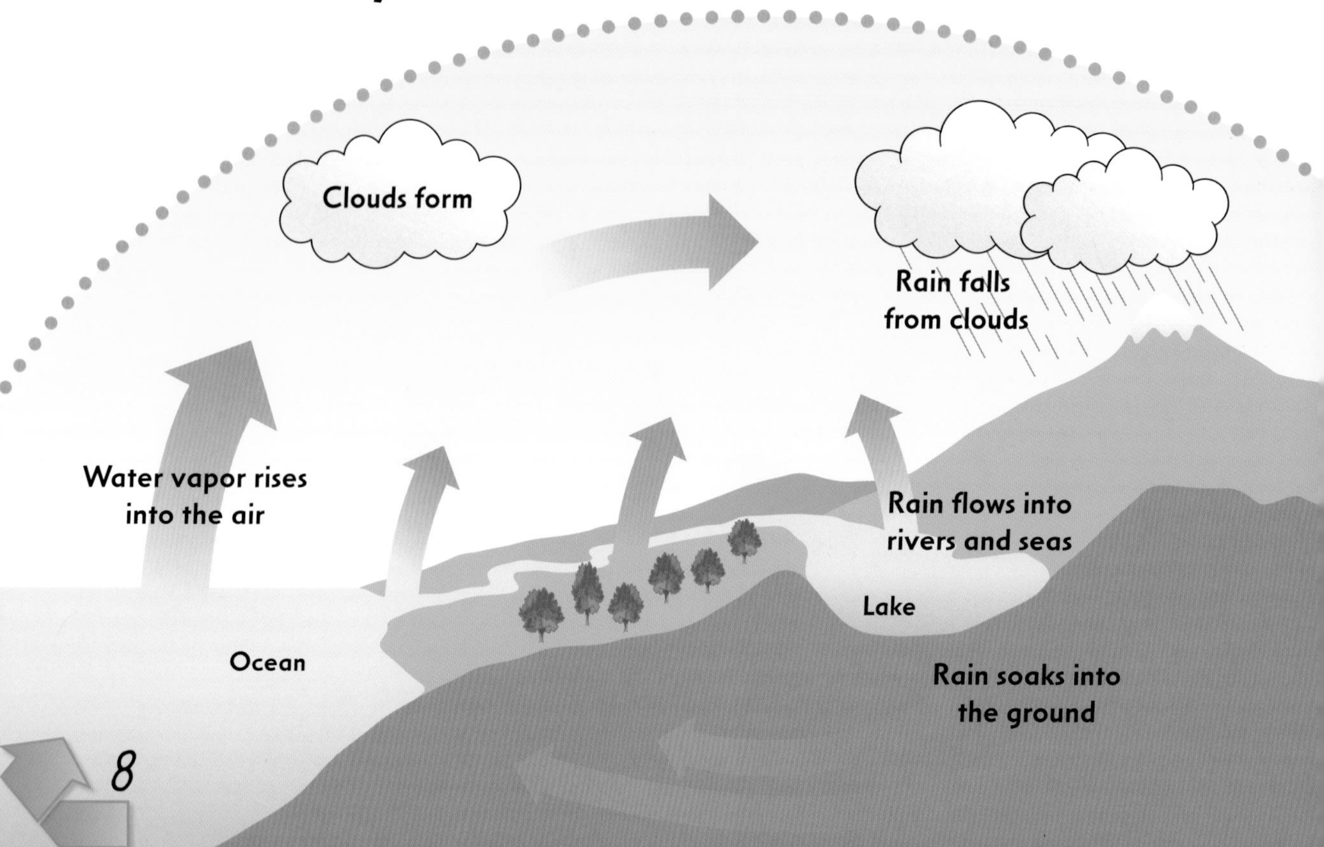

Rain that fell on dinosaurs millions of years ago is the same rain that falls today.

The heat from the sun shines on lakes, oceans, and rivers. This heat changes water into a gas called **water vapor**. The gas rises into the air and forms clouds. Clouds return water to the Earth as rain, snow, or sleet.

How Does Water Get to Our Homes?

The water that we use comes from lakes, rivers, and underground **aquifers**. Before we use water from these sources, it must be brought to a **water treatment plant**.

This is the inside of a water treatment plant.

This man is cleaning the water at a treatment plant.

At a water treatment plant, water is made clean enough to drink. The clean water is carried by underground pipes to our homes for use in sinks, baths, and showers.

Will We Always Have Water?

Water falls from clouds as rain, sleet, or snow.

Water is a **renewable resource**. It moves from the land to the clouds and back to the land again. It changes form but does not disappear.

Some parts of the world have enough water, but their water sources have become **polluted**. The water is too dirty to drink safely. Some parts of the world have very little water. They do not have enough water to drink or to grow crops.

People are trying to find ways to help those who need water.

What Happens When We Waste Water?

Water that is dumped down a sink or toilet must be cleaned at a **wastewater treatment plant**. This wastes **electricity**, a form of **energy** (power).

After dirty water is cleaned, it is returned to lakes, rivers, and streams.

If clean water is poured down the drain, it mixes with dirty water.

If we waste less water, not as much water will have to be cleaned. This will save energy.

How Can We Reduce Water Waste?

We can reduce water waste by using less water. When you get water from a faucet, pour only what you will drink. Never leave a faucet running.

Do not run water to get it cold. Instead, keep a pitcher of water in the refrigerator.

Turn off the faucet when you brush your teeth.

Use clothing and towels more than once. Washing machines use water to clean clothes and towels. If we wash items less often, we will reduce water waste.

How Can We Reuse Water?

There are many ways to reuse water. If you are not going to finish a glass of water, do not dump it down the sink. Instead, water a plant with your leftover water.

Collect rainwater in a bucket to water flowers on a hot, dry day.

Use leftover dishwater to rinse bottles and cans for **recycling**.

You can water bushes or outdoor plants with leftover dishwater. The soap left in the water will help the ground soak up the water.

What Is Recycled Water?

These tanks remove solids from dirty water.

After water is cleaned at a **wastewater treatment plant**, it is often sent back to rivers or streams. The water can be reused before it returns to that body of water. This is called **recycled** water.

Recycled water can be used to water farmland. The water soaks into the ground and then flows back to lakes, rivers, or streams.

Watering crops is a good way to use recycled water.

What Is Water Pollution?

Water **pollution** is when poisons get into the water supply. This can happen when wastes or **chemicals** are dumped into rivers or lakes. The water becomes unsafe to drink.

Polluted water can kill animals and fish.

When ships carrying oil crash, people must act fast to control the harm to plants and animals.

We must keep our water sources clean so we will always have the water we need. **Polluted** water can make people sick. It must be cleaned before it can be used.

How Can We Reduce Water Pollution?

To keep water clean, we must not add harmful things to it. Anything dumped on the ground, into the water, or down a sink or toilet can harm water.

Water from storm drains goes right into streams or rivers.

Compost can be added to soil to help plants grow.

Do not put food scraps down a sink. They **pollute** the clean water. Instead, create a **compost** pile for food scraps. A compost pile is a collection of food waste that eventually rots away.

How Can You Take Action?

You can help reduce water waste. Remind family and friends of ways to use water wisely. Make sure you use only the water you need.

Use a watering can instead of a hose to save water.

Trash needs to be picked up near bodies of water to help keep them clean.

You can help keep our water clean. Be careful not to put harmful things into the water. Never throw trash into lakes or rivers.

Does a Shower Waste Less Water Than a Bath?

The next time you take a shower, close the plug and let the water collect in the tub. When you finish your shower, see how much water is in the tub. How much water would you use for a bath?

Which uses more water, a bath or a short shower?

Fast Facts

You waste around two gallons of water each time you leave the water running while you brush your teeth.

Saltwater from the oceans can be turned into fresh drinking water by removing the salt. This is called desalting.

About 500 million people live in areas of the world where there is not enough water.

Taking a bath uses around twice as much water as taking a short shower.

Glossary

aquifer	layer of rock, sand, or gravel that holds water underground
chemical	basic element that makes up all things
compost	food scraps and plant waste that can be added to soil
electricity	form of energy used to create light and heat
energy	power to do work
pollute	harm the air, soil, or water with chemicals or wastes
pollution	wastes and poisons in the air, water, or soil
recycle	process and reuse; recycling is the process of breaking down something and using it again
renewable resource	material of the earth that can be replaced
wastewater treatment plant	place where water from sinks and toilets goes to be cleaned before it is returned to rivers and streams
water cycle	constant movement of water between sky, land, and sea
water treatment plant	place where water is taken from lakes, rivers, and streams to be cleaned for use in homes
water vapor	tiny drops of water that float in the air and form clouds

Find Out More

Books to Read

Ballard, Carol. *How We Use Water*. Chicago: Raintree, 2005.

Ditchfield, Christin. *Water*. New York: Children's Press, 2002.

Graham, Ian. *Water: A Resource Our World Depends On*. Chicago: Raintree, 2005.

Web Sites

The Environmental Protection Agency works to protect the air, water, and land. The organization has a special Web site for students at www.epa.gov/kids.

Earth911 is an organization that gives information about where you can recycle in your community. Their Web site for students is http://www.earth911.org/master.asp?s=kids&a=kids/kids.asp.

Index